Coach Black

Driven Success

How to become a Used Car Dealer FAST

This book was professionally typeset on Reedsy
Find out more at reedsy.com

Contents

1.

    1.

    2.

    3.

    4.

    5.

    6.

7.

8.

9.

10.

11.

12.

    1.

13.

14.

    1.

    2.

15.

Carving Your Niche in the Used Car Market

The used car market is a vast, ever-changing landscape, and to succeed in it, you need to identify your place and establish your niche. But how do you find your niche in a sea of dealerships and vehicles?

Well, it begins by understanding what a niche is: it's a specialized segment of the market. In the context of the used car market, a niche could be anything from budget-friendly vehicles for students to top-of-the-line luxury cars for affluent buyers. Your niche is where you focus your efforts; it's the specific types of vehicles and customers you cater to.

The first step in carving out your niche is market research. Market research involves gathering, analyzing, and interpreting information about your market, including your customers and competitors. Understanding the landscape will help you identify potential niches and assess their profitability.

Let's consider two possible niches: sports cars and budget-friendly cars. These are vastly different segments, each with unique characteristics and challenges.

Sports Cars: A High-Octane Niche

Sports cars, such as the Charger Scat Packs and other high-performance vehicles, represent a very distinct niche. The customers in this market value speed, performance, and style. They're often enthusiasts who are passionate about their vehicles and willing to spend more for the experience these cars provide.

In the sports car niche, knowing your product is crucial. Customers are likely to be knowledgeable and have specific questions about the vehicles' performance characteristics, history, and maintenance.

One great example is a used car dealership in Atlanta, "Velocity Autoplex," which successfully carved out a niche in selling used sports cars. Their secret was not just having an impressive inventory but also a deep understanding of every car they sold and the ability to connect with their customers on a personal level. They attracted their target market with events like "test drive days," creating a community around their dealership.

Budget-Friendly Cars: Maximizing Value

At the other end of the spectrum are budget-friendly cars. This niche caters to customers looking for reliable, affordable transportation. Think students, first-time car owners, or people with a tight budget. The focus here isn't on speed or luxury, but on value and reliability.

Success in this niche comes from a deep understanding of what "value" means to your customers. They want reliable vehicles that won't break down or require expensive maintenance.

An example of a dealership succeeding in this niche is "Bargain Motors" in Savannah. They offer a selection of well-maintained, pre-owned cars at affordable prices. They stand out by offering exceptional customer service and a hassle-free buying experience, addressing common concerns for buyers in this market segment.

The Luxury Line: A High-End Niche

Another distinct niche is the luxury car market. Customers in this niche are looking for high-end, prestigious brands like Mercedes, BMW, or Audi. A used luxury car can provide the status and comfort of a new luxury car at a fraction of the cost.

Carving a niche in the used luxury car market requires a deep understanding of these vehicles and the customers who buy them. It's not just about the cars; it's about the entire buying experience. The "Luxury Pre-Owned" dealership in Buckhead is a perfect example of this. They focus on high-end used cars and provide a buying experience to match, with a luxurious showroom and personalized service.

Finding Your Niche

Once you've identified potential niches, the next step is competitor analysis. Look at what other dealerships in your area are doing. What niches are they serving? Is there a gap in the market that you could fill? If you choose to enter a niche that's already served by existing dealerships,

Understanding Your Target Customer

Your target customer's understanding is critical for defining your niche. Once you've identified a potential niche, try to understand as much as possible about the customers in that segment. What are their needs and preferences? How much are they willing to spend? Where do they go to find information on used cars? The answers to these questions will help shape your marketing strategy.

In the sports car niche, for example, customers often prioritize performance, aesthetics, and brand heritage. They're likely to do extensive research before purchasing and may frequent online car enthusiast forums or social media groups. They may also attend car shows or other events where they can see and experience these vehicles in person.

In contrast, customers in the budget-friendly car niche often prioritize reliability, fuel economy, and low maintenance costs. They might be first-time car buyers or students, families needing a second car, or people trying to save money. They're likely to do their research online and may rely heavily on reviews and recommendations.

Tailoring Your Approach

With a deep understanding of your target customers, you can tailor your approach to meet their needs. This includes not only the types of cars you sell but also your marketing strategies, customer service, and even your dealership's physical layout and appearance.

For instance, if you're selling sports cars, your dealership might have a sleek, modern look that complements the high-performance vehicles you're selling. You could host events that draw in car enthusiasts, such as car shows or test drive events, and you could engage with potential customers on car enthusiast forums and social media groups.

If you're selling budget-friendly cars, your approach will be different. You might focus on creating a friendly, welcoming atmosphere that puts budget-conscious customers at ease. Your staff would need to be knowledgeable about each vehicle's reliability and cost of ownership, as these are key concerns for your customers.

Evaluating the Competition

As you refine your niche, you'll also need to evaluate your competition. Are there other dealerships serving the same niche? If so, what are they doing well, and where are they falling short? Can you differentiate yourself from them?

Let's consider the sports car niche again. If there's a dealership in your area that specializes in European sports cars, could you differentiate yourself by specializing in American-made sports cars? Or, if the competition focuses on older, classic sports cars, could you specialize in more recent models?

Alternatively, if there are already several budget-friendly car dealerships in your area, you might differentiate yourself by offering a better buying experience. Could you make the buying process more transparent, less stressful, and more friendly?

Building Relationships

Successful niche marketing is not just about selling cars; it's about building relationships. This is especially true in the used car business, where trust is paramount. You're not just selling a car; you're selling peace of mind.

This means being honest about each vehicle's condition, offering fair pricing, and standing by your cars after the sale. It means getting to know your customers, understanding their needs, and helping them find the right car for them.

For example, if you're selling sports cars, you might build relationships by attending car shows, joining online car enthusiast communities, or even hosting events at your dealership. If you're selling budget-friendly cars, you might build relationships by offering workshops on car maintenance or safe driving.

Carving your niche in the used car market is not a one-time task; it requires ongoing effort. The market changes, customer preferences evolve, and new competitors emerge. To succeed, you need to keep up with these changes, continuously refine your approach, and stay true to your niche.

In conclusion, identifying your niche is the key to standing out in the vast used car market. Whether it's sports cars, budget-friendly cars, luxury vehicles, or another segment entirely, understanding your market and your customers, tailoring your approach, evaluating your competition, and building relationships will help you carve your niche and achieve success.

Establishing Your Company Name

The business world is abuzz with brands. They are the names we associate with products, services, and the experiences that resonate with us. In your journey to becoming a successful used car dealer, your brand - your company name - will play a significant role. This chapter is dedicated to guiding you through the crucial process of establishing your company name.

The Importance of a Company Name

A company name is more than just a string of letters strung together. It's the first introduction customers have to what you offer. It sets the tone, communicates your company culture, and ultimately, becomes synonymous with your reputation.

Think about iconic names in the car dealership world, such as CarMax, AutoNation, or DriveTime. Each name, in its way, speaks volumes about the company it represents. CarMax implies they offer the maximum value or range, AutoNation conjures up an image of a vast, country-wide network of vehicles, and DriveTime suggests a focus on the experience and joy of driving.

Your company's name will be the cornerstone of your brand. It's an opportunity to make a strong first impression and start the narrative about what your dealership stands for.

Brainstorming Your Name

Coming up with a name requires a brainstorming process. Gather your team, if you have one, and get a whiteboard, sticky notes, or a blank document ready. You want a space where ideas can flow freely and be visually represented.

Begin by thinking about your mission, your niche, and your unique selling proposition. What makes your dealership stand out? What are the core values that underpin your business? Answering these questions will give you a list of words and ideas to work with.

In my own journey, I remember the excitement of this process. We were a small team with a vision to bring affordable, quality used cars to our community. Words like 'value', 'reliable', 'community', and 'trust' came up. We played with combinations, made up words, and even looked at foreign words that embodied our values. In the end, we settled on "TrustDrive." It was simple but effectively communicated our mission.

Validating Your Company Name

Once you have a list of potential names, you need to validate them. This involves several steps:

1. **Check for Uniqueness:** You want your name to stand out and not be confused with another business, especially another dealership. A quick Google search is a good start. You can also check the Georgia Secretary of State's business database.

2. **Domain Availability:** In today's digital world, you'll want a website. Check if the domain name is available for your chosen name. Websites like GoDaddy or Namecheap have easy search tools for this purpose.

3. **Trademark Issues:** You don't want to inadvertently infringe on someone else's trademark. The U.S. Patent and Trademark Office has a trademark database (TESS) you can search.

4. **Test Your Name:** Share your potential name with others to get feedback. Does it make sense? Is it easy to pronounce and spell? Does it resonate with your target audience?

One lesson I learned during this phase was not to rush. We had initially liked a different name, "ValueMotors," but further checks revealed another dealership in a neighboring state with that name. We decided to avoid potential confusion and continue our search. It was a frustrating setback, but in hindsight, it led us to a name that better fit our brand.

Tips to Make the Name Resonate

Finally, here are some tips to help make your company name resonate with your target audience:

1. **Keep it Simple:** The simpler your name, the easier it is for customers to remember

Getting Your Dealer License in Georgia

Becoming a used car dealer is more than just having an inventory of cars and a place to sell them. In the state of Georgia, as in most states, you're required to obtain a dealer's license before you can begin operations. This chapter breaks down the steps needed to get your used car dealer license in Georgia and provides a handy checklist to keep you on track.

Understand the Importance

The first step is understanding why a dealer's license is necessary. Apart from being a legal requirement, holding a dealer's license adds credibility to your dealership. It tells your customers and your competitors that you adhere to the state's business practices and ethics.

Fulfilling the Basic Requirements

Before you apply for your dealer's license, there are a few basic requirements that you need to fulfill:

1. **Establish a Business Location:** You need to have a physical location for your dealership. This location must meet zoning regulations and include an office and display area. Additionally, it should have a working telephone number listed in the business's name. If your starting small a office suite is just fine. Normally ranging in price from 300-500

dollars per month. You can find office suites all over the Atlanta area. Norcross,GA and Marietta, Ga are some major suite spots. Reach out to me if you need some referrals.

2. **Get a Sales Tax Number:** You're required to register for a sales tax number from the Georgia Department of Revenue.

3. **Acquire Liability Insurance:** Dealerships in Georgia are required to maintain liability insurance coverage.

Completing the Application

Once you've fulfilled the basic requirements, the next step is to complete your application. This involves several key components:

1. **Obtain a Surety Bond:** A surety bond is a guarantee that you will adhere to state laws and regulations. The required amount in Georgia is $35,000.

2. **Complete a Background Check:** All owners, partners, and officers are required to submit to a criminal background check.

3. **Attend a Pre-Licensing Seminar:** All used car dealer license applicants in Georgia are required to complete a four-hour pre-licensing seminar approved by the Georgia Board of Used Motor Vehicle Dealers.

4. **Complete the Application Form:** Fill in the Used Motor Vehicle Dealer Application, making sure to provide all the required information. Double-check your entries to avoid unnecessary delays.

Remember when I was applying for my dealership license? I recall my application being delayed due to an oversight in the form. I had left a section of the form incomplete. The delay cost me a couple of weeks and added unnecessary stress to the process. I learned a valuable lesson - always double-check your application form!

Await Approval (2-6 months)

Once you submit your application along with the required fees, the Georgia Used Motor Vehicle Division will review it. They take their sweet time. While waiting for approval your bills are still due, so aspect this from the start. You need money to get into this business. If your application is approved, they will send a representative for an on-site inspection of your dealership location.

This was another point in my journey where I learned a valuable lesson. When the representative came for the inspection, I was away, thinking my assistant could handle it. However, the inspector wanted to verify some specifics with me. This resulted in another delay. Lesson learned – ensure you're present for the inspection.

A Checklist for Your Convenience

Here's a handy checklist summarizing the steps and requirements for getting your used car dealer license in Georgia:

1. Establish a business location that meets zoning regulations
2. Obtain a sales tax number from the Georgia Department of Revenue
3. Acquire liability insurance for your dealership
4. Get a $35,000 surety bond
5. Complete a criminal background check for all owners, partners, and officers
6. Attend a pre-licensing seminar approved by the Georgia Board of Used Motor Vehicle Dealers
7. Fill out the Used Motor Vehicle Dealer Application

8. Submit your application with the required fees and wait for approval

Keep this checklist handy and refer to it throughout your application process. A well-prepared application can help

"It's almost like running a marathon before the race even begins, isn't it? You go through all this work of setting up your business, getting insured, attending a seminar, going through background checks, filling out paperwork, and you haven't even sold a car yet. But hey, who said the road to 'auto'matic success was a highway? Sometimes it starts with a bit of off-roading!"

Remember, while these steps may seem arduous, they're your path to a successful and legally sound car dealership. So gear up, buckle in, and enjoy the ride to becoming a licensed used car dealer in   Georgia!

Mistakes I Made and How I Overcame Them: A Personal Journey

Running a used car dealership is a thrilling, high-stakes journey. Like any entrepreneurial endeavor, it's filled with its fair share of bumps and detours. In this chapter, I'll take you through some of the significant mistakes I made when I first started my dealership and how I overcame them.

Mistake 1: Ignoring Online Presence

When I first started my used car dealership, I was convinced that the traditional method of selling cars through a physical location was all I needed. I believed in the old-school method of face-to-face interactions. How wrong I was! For all you suite dealers you can relate. You have not lot, so your online presence is essential.

As months passed, I noticed that many potential customers were going to dealerships that had a robust online presence. I realized that in the digital age, customers like to research online before stepping into a dealership.

Overcoming the Mistake

I quickly understood the importance of an online presence and took immediate action. I invested in building a website for my dealership, which provided essential details about our inventory, contact information, and our unique selling proposition.

Additionally, we began using social media platforms to connect with our customers more effectively. We regularly posted about our latest vehicles, engaged with potential buyers, and created a community around our brand.

Instagram became a crucial part of our online strategy. Here's a tip: Don't hesitate to make your posts personal. You can share images and videos of cars you currently have, or even those you aspire to have in your lot in the future. Adding special effects or music to your posts helps them stand out, attracting more attention.

Remember, it's perfectly acceptable to project your ambitions on social media. As the saying goes, sometimes you have to **"fake it until you make it"**. The key is to be catchy and flashy. Craft posts that grab attention, stir interest, and showcase not just your inventory, but also the unique personality of your dealership.

Lesson Learned

The modern customer is digital-first. A strong online presence can enhance visibility, boost credibility, and drive more traffic to your business.

Mistake 2: Not Knowing Enough About the Cars I Was Selling

In my initial days as a dealer, I was not knowledgeable enough about the used cars I was selling. I trusted the assessments of the sellers without doing my own research. This ignorance led to a couple of instances where I sold cars with hidden problems. These issues damaged my reputation when frustrated customers had to deal with unexpected repairs.

Overcoming the Mistake

I decided to educate myself. I learned about different car models, their common issues, and maintenance needs. I started doing thorough checks of every car that came into my dealership, hiring a skilled mechanic to ensure all vehicles were in good condition before selling them.

Lesson Learned

Knowledge is power in the used car business. Being an expert about the cars you sell can help you avoid problematic vehicles, protect your reputation, and provide better service to your customers.

Mistake 3: Neglecting Customer Relationships

At the start, I was focused purely on selling. I did not take the time to build relationships with my customers, missing out on the potential for repeat business and referrals.

Overcoming the Mistake

I shifted my focus to building strong relationships with my customers. I started following up with them after their purchase, asking for their feedback, and addressing any issues they faced. I also started a referral program to reward customers who brought in new business.

Lesson Learned

Building relationships with customers can lead to loyalty, repeat business, and valuable referrals. It's not just about the initial sale, but creating a lasting relationship.

Mistake 4: Not Keeping Up With Market Trends

In my early years, I underestimated the importance of keeping up with market trends. I stocked vehicles that I thought were good sellers, only to discover that consumer preferences had changed.

Overcoming the Mistake

I started subscribing to auto industry publications, attending car shows, and staying informed about the latest trends. This knowledge allowed me to stock vehicles that were in demand and stay ahead of the competition.

Lesson Learned

Understanding and keeping up with market trends is crucial in the used car business. It helps you know which vehicles to stock, what prices to set, and how to market them effectively.

Remember, the road to success is paved with mistakes. However, each mistake is an opportunity to learn and improve. It's these lessons that shape your journey, driving you closer to your destination.

Know the Deal Breakers - Factors That Can Make You Ineligible

Before you set out on the journey to becoming a used car dealer, it's important to understand the various requirements and potential disqualifiers that can throw a wrench in your plans. This chapter will outline some of the crucial prerequisites and deal-breakers that you need to be aware of before you start your dealership.

Criminal Record

A clean criminal record is a must for all applicants for a dealer's license in Georgia. Having a felony or certain misdemeanor convictions can potentially disqualify you from becoming a dealer. I remember how nerve-wracking it was waiting for my background check to come through, knowing that any overlooked incidents could halt my dream.

Proper Zoning

Having a proper place to operate your business is critical. But not just any location will do. Your dealership needs to be situated in an area that is correctly zoned for a car dealership. Ignoring this requirement can lead to heavy fines and could potentially disqualify you from becoming a dealer. Good thing is that most office suites are in the zone location. So your covered.

Insufficient Funds

Starting a used car dealership requires significant capital. Undercapitalization is one of the primary reasons new businesses fail. Not only will you need money for inventory and a location, but you also have to consider ongoing expenses like utilities, salaries, insurance, and marketing. A lack of sufficient funds can be a significant barrier to entering the dealership business.

Lack of a Surety Bond

In Georgia, you're required to obtain a surety bond of $35,000 before you can get your dealer's license. This is to protect customers from fraudulent or unethical dealers. If you are unable or unwilling to secure this bond, it can be a deal breaker for your dealership aspirations. Remember, this does not mean you have to have $35,000. You only need the bond. This can range from 300 dollars per year with good credit up to a few thousand dollars if your credit is bad. The most I ever heard of a $35,000 was $3,000. But the average I have seen has been $400 -$600.

Failure to Complete a Pre-Licensing Seminar

Before you can get your dealer's license in Georgia, you must complete a pre-licensing seminar. This course is essential in providing you with the information you need to successfully run your dealership. Skipping this step can not only disqualify you from getting your license, but also leave you unprepared to manage your dealership. You can find these classes for about $199 or less most places charges $125.

Non-compliance with State Laws and Regulations

As a used car dealer, you are required to comply with all state laws and regulations. This includes everything from adhering to fair business practices to ensuring your vehicles meet safety and emissions standards. Failure to comply with these laws and regulations can lead to fines, license suspension, or even disqualification.

Checklist to Ensure Eligibility

To help ensure you meet all the necessary requirements and avoid any potential deal-breakers, here's a handy checklist:

1. Clean Criminal Record: Make sure your record is free of any disqualifying offenses.

2. Proper Zoning: Ensure your business location is zoned for a car dealership.
3. Sufficient Funds: Have a robust business plan outlining all costs, demonstrating your financial preparedness.
4. Surety Bond: Obtain a $35,000 surety bond from a reputable provider.
5. Pre-Licensing Seminar: Complete the state-approved seminar before applying for your license.
6. Compliance with Laws and Regulations: Familiarize yourself with state laws and regulations, ensuring your dealership adheres to them.

Remember, launching a successful dealership requires more than just a passion for cars. You must meet certain legal and procedural prerequisites to even get started. Understanding these potential deal-breakers can save you time, money, and heartache down the line. So buckle up, do your due diligence, and steer clear of these roadblocks on your path to becoming a used car dealer. Remember this quote: "Takes money to make money."

Choosing the Perfect Cars to Start Selling

Choosing the right cars to start selling at your dealership is a bit like trying to pick a winning horse at the races. You can study the stats, listen to the pundits, but at the end of the day, it's a little bit of luck and a whole lot of skill. And trust me, there's no joy quite like watching your chosen "horse"—or in our case, car—cross the finish line first, making a profitable sale.

So, how do you go about selecting these automotive steeds? What's the secret formula?

Understanding Market Trends

The first step in choosing the right cars is to understand the market trends. Just as bell-bottoms had their heyday in the 70s but wouldn't sell well today (unless you're targeting hipsters), certain car models are hot commodities in one decade and old news in the next.

So, start by doing your research. Subscribe to auto industry publications, browse online car forums, and don't forget to attend car shows.

Identifying Customer Preferences

This one's a no-brainer. What does your target customer want? If you're catering to the luxury market, you won't get far selling minivans, no matter how 'luxurious' they may be. Similarly, if your customers are budget-conscious families, high-end sports cars might just gather dust on your lot.

For me, my target audience was working-class families looking for reliable, budget-friendly cars. Sure, a Ferrari or Lamborghini might turn heads, but they wouldn't turn profits for me.

Profitability

Here's where we talk about the moolah. Now, you might think that higher-priced cars mean higher profits. But remember, in the used car business, it's not just about the selling price; it's also about the buying price and costs of refurbishment. You make your money buying.

The average profit per car in the used car industry ranges between $1,000 and $1,500. To hit those numbers, you need to buy low, refurbish smart, and sell at the right price. This is where understanding the 'Black Book' value comes in handy. The 'Black Book' is a dealer-only resource that provides wholesale values of used cars, helping you make profitable buying decisions. If you buying from auctions like Manhiem you got the MMR which means Mahiem market

Sourcing Quality Cars

Alright, you've got the knowledge, you've got the customer preferences down, and you're ready to make a profit. Now, where do you find these cars? There are various sources – auctions, private sales, or trade-ins. Each has its pros and cons, and the key is to balance cost with quality.

Choosing Cars Easier to Finance

Choosing cars that are easier to finance can increase your customer base and, therefore, your sales. Certain makes and models have better finance rates due to their reliability, resale value, and demand.

For instance, many lenders love financing Honda Civics or Toyota Camrys because they have a proven track record of reliability, hold their value well, and have a steady demand. So don't just think about the cars you love—think about the cars finance companies love, too!

Checklist to Choose the Right Cars

1. Market Research: Know the latest trends and most popular models.
2. Identify Target Customer: Understand what your target customer wants.
3. Profitability: Know your costs and potential profits for each car.
4. Sourcing: Identify reliable sources for quality cars.
5. Financing: Consider the ease of financing for different car models.

Remember, choosing the right car to sell is a mix of science, art, and a bit of gut instinct. It's like dating—you have to find the perfect match, know when to invest,

Building a Strong Business Plan

Ah, the business plan. The mere mention of it can send shivers down the spine of many an entrepreneur. It's a bit like cleaning out your garage. You know it's necessary, you know it will be beneficial, but the thought of actually doing it can be daunting.

However, just like that garage, once you clear the clutter and get it in order, you'll have a much easier time finding what you need. So, let's roll up our sleeves, turn up that old-school rock playlist (I'm partial to some classic Queen myself), and get down to business.

Mission Statement

This is like the dealership's superhero catchphrase. It's your "To infinity and beyond!" or "With great power comes great responsibility." It's a succinct statement that captures the essence of your business and its values.

When I was creating my mission statement, I envisioned it as a billboard advertising my dealership. It read, "Delivering Reliable Rides at Reasonable Rates." That became my compass, guiding every business decision I made.

Market Analysis

This is your chance to play detective. You'll need to investigate the used car market, identify key trends, understand your competitors, and pinpoint your target customer.

Consider it your dealership's treasure map. X marks your customer, and you need to find the best path to reach them, navigating around competitors and adapting to the market terrain.

Marketing and Sales Strategy

This is your battle plan. It outlines how you will attract customers to your dealership and convince them to buy your cars.

For me, my marketing strategy was a mix of digital wizardry and good old-fashioned networking. My website was my digital showroom, social media my megaphone, and every local event, my chance to shake hands and win hearts.

Financial Projections

Now, we're talking about the big bucks. This section is where you crunch the numbers and forecast your financial future.

Picture yourself as a fortune teller, gazing into a crystal ball. But instead of vague prophecies, you're making educated predictions based on data and calculations. This section will cover your initial investment, ongoing costs, projected sales, and anticipated profit.

Let me tell you, staring at spreadsheets and wrestling with numbers was never my cup of tea. But a bit of patience, lots of coffee, and some late-night number-crunching sessions helped me chart a financial path for my business.

Checklist to Craft Your Business Plan

1. Catchy Mission Statement: Create a powerful phrase that captures your dealership's essence.
2. Comprehensive Market Analysis: Do your detective work and understand the market inside out.

3. Effective Marketing and Sales Strategy: Craft a battle plan to attract and win customers.

4. Accurate Financial Projections: Play fortune teller and predict your financial future.

Remember, creating a business plan isn't just a tedious task to tick off your startup checklist. It's your roadmap to success. And like any road trip, it's always more enjoyable with some good tunes, a bit of laughter, and the anticipation of reaching your destination—owning a   successful   used   car   dealership

Finding the Right Location

If there's one thing that the world of real estate and used car dealerships have in common, it's this golden rule; location, location, location! Selecting the right location for your dealership is a bit like choosing the perfect parking spot at a packed concert. Too far away, and no one will bother walking all the way to you; too close to the rowdy crowd, and you're asking for trouble.

Zoning Laws

The first thing you need to consider when scouting for your dealership's location are the zoning laws. Zoning laws are like your Mom when you were a teenager—they dictate where you can go, what you can do, and when you can do it. So, before you fall in love with a location, make sure it's zoned for a used car dealership.

Traffic Patterns

Next up, traffic patterns. You want your dealership to be visible and easy to access. So, select a location where there's a lot of vehicle and foot traffic. It's like setting up your lemonade stand at a bustling intersection instead of a quiet cul-de-sac.

But remember, all traffic is not created equal. Pay attention to the direction of the traffic. If most of the traffic is heading out of town in the morning and coming back in the evening, you might have a captive audience for your morning and evening advertisements.

Customer Demographics

You know who your target customer is; now, it's time to find out where they hang out. Choosing a location that's convenient for your target demographic will make it easier for them to visit your dealership.

For instance, if your target customers are families, you might want to consider a location near residential neighborhoods, schools, or shopping centers. If your customers are high-end sports car enthusiasts, a location near upscale dining or shopping districts could work well.

The Broker's Suite

Now, if you're a broker and don't plan to maintain a physical inventory, your requirements might be a bit different. You might not need a sprawling lot by the highway; instead, a smaller office space in a professional building might suit your needs better. Call it the "Broker's Suite."

Regardless, the location still matters. While your customers might not be visiting to browse through rows of cars, they'll appreciate a convenient, accessible location with ample parking.

When I started my dealership, I spent countless hours driving around, scouting locations, and crunching numbers. In the end, I found a location that was not just good but perfect—it was visible, accessible, and right smack in the middle of my target demographic.

Finding the right location for your dealership might take some time, but remember—it's not just a place to park your inventory; it's the stage where you'll showcase your cars, win your customers, and build your business. So take your time, do your research, and keep that sense of humor handy because the road to finding your ideal location might be long and winding, but the destination will be worth it.

Navigating Legal Landscapes

Ah, legal landscapes. They're a bit like those corn mazes you find at fall festivals—confusing, complex, and enough to give even the bravest souls a scare. But just as with those mazes, there's a way through the tangle of laws and regulations—you just need the right guidance and a bit of patience.

Dealer Laws

First things first, dealer laws. These are like the commandments of the used car dealership world. Break them, and you're in for a world of trouble. Obey them, and you're on your way to running a successful, above-board operation.

Dealer laws cover a range of topics, from how to obtain and maintain your license, to the rules around vehicle titles, to requirements for warranty disclosures. It's like learning a whole new language—legal-ese.

Customer Rights

If dealer laws are commandments, customer rights are the golden rules. They protect your customers and ensure that they're treated fairly. As a dealer, it's not just your job to know these rights; it's your duty to uphold them.

Customer rights cover areas such as financing, warranties, and fair advertising. And remember, breaking these rules isn't just bad for your customers—it's bad for business. The last thing you want is a reputation for shady dealings.

Legal Advisor

Here's where the role of a legal advisor comes in. They're like your GPS in the maze of legal landscapes. And let me tell you, having a good one on your side can make all the difference.

When I started my dealership, I thought I could handle all the legalities on my own. But boy, was I wrong! I remember once, I ended up in a tight spot due to a misunderstanding around a warranty disclosure. It was like I had walked into a den of lions, armed with nothing more than a spoon.

It was my legal advisor who helped me navigate that tricky situation, armed with her knowledge and sharp legal acumen. She was like the superhero who swooped in, just in time, and saved the day.

So, take it from me, invest in a good legal advisor. It's not an expense; it's an insurance policy for your business.

Legal Landscapes Checklist

1. Know Your Dealer Laws: Make sure you understand and follow all dealer laws.
2. Uphold Customer Rights: Know what rights your customers have and ensure you uphold them.
3. Hire a Legal Advisor: They are your guiding star in the legal landscape.

Remember, navigating the legal landscape of the used car industry can feel like walking through a minefield with a blindfold on. But with the right knowledge, a solid legal advisor, and a healthy dose of humor, you can not only survive but thrive. Because at the end of the day, the rule of law is the rule of business. And those who play by the   rules,   win.

Crafting Your Marketing and Sales Strategies

Welcome to the exciting world of marketing and sales, the one-two punch of running a successful used car dealership. Think of it like dating—you need to make a great first impression (that's marketing) and then charm your date into saying 'yes' (that's sales).

Marketing: Wooing Your Customers

Before you can sell your cars, you need to attract customers to your dealership, and that's where marketing comes in. Marketing is a bit like fishing—you've got to find the right bait and know where to cast your line.

Traditional Marketing

Just because we're in the digital age doesn't mean we should forget the tried-and-true methods of yesteryears. Signs, billboards, local newspaper ads, and radio spots can still be effective, especially in smaller towns. It's like sending a postcard in an age of emails—there's something charmingly nostalgic about it that catches the eye.

Digital Marketing

Welcome to the World Wide Web, where potential customers are just a click away. A well-designed website, regular social media posts, and email newsletters can do wonders for your dealership.

Your website is your digital storefront. Make sure it's as polished and welcoming as your physical location. Social media is your chance to showcase your inventory, share customer testimonials, and engage with potential buyers. It's like hosting a party where everyone's invited, and the main attraction is your cars.

And email newsletters? They're like a friendly catch-up over coffee, a way to stay in touch and keep your dealership top-of-mind.

Search Engine Optimization (SEO)

SEO is like the magic spell of the digital world. It helps you become more visible on search engines, which can lead to more website visits and, ultimately, more sales. SEO can be a complex beast, but don't worry—you don't need to be a wizard to use it. There are plenty of resources and tools available to help you harness the power of SEO.

Sales: Sealing the Deal

Once you've lured customers to your dealership, it's time to seal the deal. Sales strategies are like your playbook in a high-stakes game of football. You've got the ball (the customer), and now you need to run it to the end zone (the sale).

Build Relationships, Not Just Sales

People buy from people, not businesses. Building a relationship with your customers can make the difference between a one-time sale and a loyal customer. It's like planting a garden. You need to cultivate it with care and patience to see it bloom.

Remember, the car buying process can be stressful for many people. Be their guide, their confidante, their trusted advisor. Show them that you're not just interested in their wallet, but in helping them find the right car.

Customer Relationship Management (CRM) Systems

A CRM system is like your personal assistant, keeping track of your customer interactions and helping you manage relationships more effectively. It can remind you to follow up with potential buyers, alert you to service dates for existing customers, and provide valuable data to help you refine your sales strategies. It's not just a tool—it's your secret weapon in the sales game.

Remember, crafting your marketing and sales strategies isn't just a box to tick—it's a crucial component of your dealership's success. With the right mix of traditional and digital marketing, a focus on relationship building, and the effective use of tools like CRM systems, you can attract more customers, close more deals, and drive your dealership to success.

Just remember, marketing and sales are like a dance. It takes time to learn the steps, and you might step on a few toes along the way (I know I did!).

The Right DMS

A Dealer Management System is like the command center of your dealership. It's a software system that helps you manage everything from inventory control and sales processes to accounting and customer relationships. Think of it as your Swiss Army knife for dealership management.

Now, let's take a look at two popular DMS systems in the market:

Dealer Center

Dealer Center (website: www.dealercenter.com) is a robust DMS that provides an all-in-one solution for your dealership. It's like the Swiss watch of DMS systems—sophisticated, efficient, and reliable.

With Dealer Center, you can manage your inventory, process sales, and even run credit reports. It also offers integrated marketing tools to help you reach potential customers and CRM features to keep track of your customer interactions. It's like having a trusty sidekick that's got your back.

Wayne Reaves

Another strong contender in the DMS market is Wayne Reaves (website: www.waynereaves.com). Their software offers a comprehensive suite of features for managing your dealership, from inventory and sales to accounting and financing.

Wayne Reaves is like that versatile kitchen gadget that slices, dices, and even makes your morning coffee. It's designed to streamline your operations and boost productivity, giving you more time to focus on what matters—selling cars and building relationships with your customers.

Apart from Dealer Center and Wayne Reaves, there are other DMS providers in the market, like Frazer (www.frazer.com) and Auto/Mate (www.automate.com), each with its own set of features and benefits.

Choosing a DMS is like finding the perfect car—it should fit your needs, be reliable, and within your budget. So, do your research, take them for a test drive, and find the one that's the perfect match for your dealership.

Remember, a good DMS isn't an expense—it's an investment in your dealership's efficiency and growth. So, choose wisely and let your DMS take the wheel of your dealership operations. After all, even the best drivers need a co-pilot.

Managing Finances and Growth

Alright folks, buckle up! We're about to dive into the thrilling rollercoaster ride that is financial management and growth. It's a bit like dieting - there are numbers involved, it's essential for a healthy business, and it's something we often wish we could avoid, but we just can't.

Managing Finances: More Fun than a Barrel of Crabs (Trust Me)

Budgeting

Budgeting is as thrilling as watching paint dry, but as necessary as having wheels on your cars. It's about knowing what's coming in, what's going out, and what's hiding under the seat. A well-structured budget is the roadmap to your financial success. It helps you identify areas where you can cut costs (bye-bye, expensive coffee machine) and where you need to invest more (hello, digital marketing).

Cash Flow

Cash flow is the lifeblood of your dealership. It's like your business's circulatory system, pumping money in and out to keep everything running smoothly. To maintain a healthy cash flow, you need to juggle incoming cash from car sales, financing deals, and outgoing cash for purchases, overheads, and that coffee you can't start your day without. Remember, a clogged cash flow can lead to a business heart attack, so keep it healthy.

Inventory Management

Your inventory is like your very own used car buffet. Too much, and you're wasting resources. Too little, and your customers leave hungry. Tracking what cars sell quickly and which ones sit around like lazy teenagers on a summer break helps you make informed decisions about what to stock. If you a car that won't sell don't panic time to take it back to auction and get a new one.

Growth: Scaling the Business Mountain

Financial Forecasting

Financial forecasting is like peeking into a crystal ball. It lets you predict future revenues and expenses based on past trends and current data. It's not about precise predictions—let's leave that to the weather forecasters—but about providing an idea of what lies ahead, so you can steer your business in the right direction.

Growth Strategies

If managing finances is dieting, then growth strategies are your fitness plan. It's about toning your business muscles and increasing its endurance. This could involve expanding your inventory, opening new locations, or even franchising your brand. The key is to grow sustainably, like a well-tended plant, not wildly, like my cousin's backyard weeds.

Remember, managing finances and planning for growth is like choreographing a dance. It requires balance, coordination, and a good sense of rhythm. But with the right moves, you can waltz your way to business success. And remember, even if you step on a few toes or stumble along the way, keep dancing. Every misstep is just a new step to learn.

So, embrace the thrill of managing your finances and pursuing growth. It may have its ups and downs, twists and turns, but it's all part of the exhilarating journey of running a used car dealership. Just remember to keep your sense of humor intact, stay on top of your numbers, and be open to adapting your strategies along the way. With a little laughter, a lot of determination, and a keen eye on your financial health, you'll be well-equipped to navigate the twists and turns of managing your finances and propelling your dealership toward long-term growth and success.

Final Checklist and Words of Encouragement

Congratulations, my fellow aspiring used car dealer! You've made it to the final chapter of this wild ride. You've braved the twists, turns, and occasional detours of the used car dealership journey. Now, as we near the finish line, let's recap the key steps and requirements with a handy-dandy checklist. But before we dive into that, let me leave you with some words of encouragement and advice—wrapped in a coating of humor, of course!

The Final Checklist: Your Roadmap to Success

1. **Business Name**: Choose a catchy and memorable name that resonates with your target audience.
2. **Licenses**: Obtain the necessary licenses and permits, including the used car dealer license in the state of GA.
3. **Location**: Find the perfect spot for your dealership, considering zoning laws, traffic patterns, and customer demographics.
4. **Business Plan**: Craft a robust business plan that includes your mission statement, market analysis, marketing and sales strategies, and financial projections.

5. **Inventory**: Choose the perfect mix of cars to sell, considering market trends, customer preferences, profitability, and financing options.

6. **Legal Compliance**: Understand and adhere to dealer laws, customer rights, and other legal requirements.

7. **Marketing and Sales**: Woo your customers with effective marketing strategies, both traditional and digital, and seal the deal with strong sales techniques and relationship building.

8. **Financial Management**: Budget wisely, manage your cash flow, track your inventory, and plan for growth through financial forecasting and sound business strategies.

9. **DMS and Tools**: Consider utilizing a Dealer Management System (DMS) like Dealer Center, Wayne Reaves, or other reputable options to streamline your operations.

10. **Sense of Humor**: Keep your sense of humor intact! Laughter is the fuel that will keep you going through the inevitable bumps in the road.

Words of Encouragement: Keep Calm and Rev Your Engines

Now, my fellow dealer-in-training, let me impart some pearls of wisdom as you embark on your used car dealership journey:

1. Embrace the Mistakes: Mistakes are like potholes on the road of entrepreneurship—they're unavoidable. But here's the secret: Embrace them! Learn from them, grow from them, and let them guide you towards greater success. Remember, even the best drivers stall now and then.

2. Seek Guidance: You don't have to navigate this road alone. Seek guidance from experienced dealers, mentors, and professionals in the industry. They've already been down this road and can provide valuable insights and advice. And remember, asking for directions isn't a sign of weakness—it's a sign of wisdom.

3. Stay Customer-Centric: Your customers are the fuel that keeps your dealership running. Treat them like royalty—provide exceptional service, be transparent, and build lasting relationships. Happy customers become repeat customers and champions of your business.

4. Adapt and Innovate: The used car market is always evolving, so be ready to adapt and innovate. Keep an eye on emerging trends, embrace new technologies, and be open to trying new approaches. Stay ahead of the curve, and you'll leave your competitors in the dust.

5. Enjoy the Ride: Yes, the road can be bumpy, and the journey might have its challenges, but remember to enjoy the ride. Celebrate the victories, savor the small wins, and find joy in the journey itself. After all, the destination is just a single moment, but the journey—that's where the memories are made.

So, my fellow used car dealer extraordinaire, get ready to rev your engines and hit the road with confidence. With

Mastering the Art of Auction Shopping and Public Options

Welcome to the exciting world of auction shopping, where cars of all makes and models go under the hammer, and dealers like you have the chance to snag some great deals. Whether you're a seasoned auction-goer or a novice in search of insider tips, this chapter will guide you through the best ways to shop at auctions as a dealer, and we'll also explore public options and the ever-expanding world of online marketplaces like Facebook Marketplace.

Understanding the Auction Landscape

Auctions are like the Grand Bazaar of the car world. They bring together dealers, individuals, and fleet owners looking to sell their vehicles quickly and efficiently. But to navigate this bustling marketplace, you'll need to arm yourself with knowledge and a strategic approach.

Research is Key

Before attending an auction, do your homework. Research the auction house or organization hosting the event. Check their reputation, past sales records, and customer reviews. You want to make sure you're dealing with a reputable auction that operates transparently and provides accurate vehicle information.

Set Your Budget and Stick to It

Auctions can be exhilarating, with bidding wars and the adrenaline rush of trying to secure a great deal. But remember, you're running a business, and financial discipline is crucial. Set a budget before you step onto the auction floor and stick to it. It's like having a strict diet plan in the land of tempting desserts—discipline is key to maintaining your financial health.

Inspect, Inspect, Inspect

At auctions, the clock is ticking, and decisions need to be made quickly. While you may not have the luxury of a lengthy inspection, it's vital to gather as much information as possible about the vehicles you're interested in. Perform a visual inspection, check the vehicle history report, and if possible, get a mechanic to conduct a pre-auction inspection. Remember, knowledge is power, and it can save you from purchasing a lemon that ends up costing you more in repairs.

Bidding Strategies

Bidding at an auction is like playing a high-stakes poker game. It's a delicate balance between being assertive and not overpaying for a car. Set your maximum bid in advance and stick to it. Stay calm, read the room, and bid strategically. Sometimes, the best move is to let a car go and wait for the next opportunity. Patience is a virtue in the auction world.

Public Options: A Hidden Gem

While auctions can be a haven for dealers, don't overlook public options. Public auctions, like government surplus sales or fleet vehicle auctions, can offer a wide range of vehicles at competitive prices. These events often have less competition from dealers, giving you a chance to snag a great deal. Keep an eye out for local public options and seize the opportunity to diversify your inventory.

Expanding Your Horizons with Online Marketplaces

The rise of online marketplaces, like Facebook Marketplace, has revolutionized the way people buy and sell cars. As a dealer, this presents a fantastic opportunity to expand your reach and tap into a vast pool of potential customers. Take advantage of these platforms to showcase your inventory, engage with buyers, and build your online presence. It's like having a digital showroom that's open 24/7.

A Word of Caution

While auctions and online marketplaces offer exciting opportunities, it's crucial to remain cautious. As with any marketplace, there may be unscrupulous sellers or misrepresented vehicles. Always conduct due diligence, perform thorough inspections, and rely on trusted sources of information.

Final Thoughts: Auction Mastery and Expanding Your Reach

Auctions and public options can be treasure troves for dealers seeking quality used cars at competitive prices. By mastering the art

Certainly! Here's a list of commonly used terms in the used car dealership industry and their meanings, as well as a list of auctions in the state of Georgia:

Used Car Dealership Terms:

1. **Wholesale**: The sale of vehicles to other dealers rather than to individual consumers.

2. **Retail**: The sale of vehicles directly to consumers.
3. **Trade-In**: A vehicle that a customer offers as part of the payment for another vehicle.
4. **Inventory**: The collection of vehicles a dealership has for sale.
5. **Title**: A legal document that proves ownership of a vehicle.
6. **MSRP**: Stands for Manufacturer's Suggested Retail Price, which is the price suggested by the vehicle manufacturer for the vehicle.
7. **Negotiation**: The process of discussing and reaching an agreement on the terms of a vehicle sale.
8. **F&I**: Stands for Finance and Insurance, which includes the financing options and insurance products offered to customers.
9. **Upside Down**: When a customer owes more on their current vehicle than its trade-in value.
10. **Lease**: A financial arrangement in which a customer pays for the use of a vehicle for a specific period of time.

Auction Terminology (According to Manheim):

1. **Lane**: The specific area at an auction where vehicles are presented for bidding.
2. **Block**: The raised platform or stage where the auctioneer stands and vehicles are driven for bidding.
3. **Hammer Price**: The final price at which a vehicle is sold when the auctioneer's hammer falls.
4. **Reserve Price**: The minimum price set by the seller at which they are willing to sell the vehicle.

5. **Run Number**: The assigned number that represents the order in which a vehicle will be auctioned.

6. **Condition Report**: A document that provides a detailed assessment of the vehicle's condition, highlighting any damages or issues.

7. **Ramp**: The area where vehicles are driven onto the auction block for bidding.

8. **Floor Price**: The starting price set by the auctioneer for bidding on a vehicle.

9. **Buy Fee**: The fee charged by the auction to the buyer for purchasing a vehicle.

10. **Seller Fee**: The fee charged by the auction to the seller for selling a vehicle.

Understanding the Lights System at Used Dealer Auction

Sure. The light system at used dealer auctions is a way to communicate the condition of a vehicle to potential buyers. The lights are displayed above the auctioneer's podium, and they are typically green, yellow, or red.

- **Green light:** A green light indicates that the vehicle is being sold in good condition and is covered by the auction's arbitration policy. This means that if the buyer finds a problem with the vehicle after they buy it, they can file a claim with the auction and have the problem repaired or compensated for.

- **Yellow light:** A yellow light indicates that the vehicle has some known defects. These defects may or may not be covered by the auction's arbitration policy. The auctioneer will usually announce the specific defects when they sell the vehicle.
- **Red light:** A red light indicates that the vehicle is being sold "as is". This means that the buyer is responsible for any problems with the vehicle, and they cannot file a claim with the auction.

It is important to pay attention to the light system when you are bidding on a vehicle at an auction. The light will tell you about the condition of the vehicle and what your rights are as a buyer.

Here are some additional things to keep in mind about the light system:

- The light system is not always consistent from auction to auction. Some auctions may use different colors for the lights, or they may have different policies about what is covered by arbitration.
- It is always a good idea to read the auction's terms and conditions before you bid on a vehicle. This will give you a better understanding of the auction's policies and what your rights are as a buyer.
- If you are not sure about the condition of a vehicle, it is always a good idea to have it inspected by a mechanic before you buy it.

List of Auctions

1. **Manheim Georgia** - Location: Atlanta, GA
2. **Manheim Atlanta** - Location: Atlanta, GA
3. **Copart Atlanta East** - Location: Loganville, GA
4. **America's Auto Auction Atlanta** - Location: College Park, GA
5. **Adesa Atlanta** - Location: Fairburn, GA
6. **Southeastern Auto Auction of Savannah** - Location: Savannah, GA
7. **AutoNation Auto Auction Atlanta** - Location: Atlanta, GA
8. **CarMax Auctions** - Location: Newnan, GA

These auctions offer a wide variety of used cars, trucks, SUVs, and vans from different manufacturers. You can find both wholesale and retail vehicles at these auctions, so there's something for everyone.

Here are some of the benefits of buying a car at a used dealer auction:

- You can often find great deals on vehicles at auctions.
- You have the opportunity to inspect the vehicle before you buy it.
- You can buy vehicles that are not available at dealerships.

However, there are also some risks associated with buying a car at an auction:

- You may not be able to test drive the vehicle before you buy it.
- You may not be able to get financing for the vehicle.
- The vehicle may have hidden damage.

If you're considering buying a car at a used dealer auction, it's important to do your research and be prepared. You should also have a pre-approved loan before you go to the auction

Hot Wheels: Top-Selling Used Cars That Drive Off the Lot

Here is an overview of why buying certain cars for a used car dealership is best:

- **Popularity:** Popular cars are more likely to be in demand, which means that they will sell for a higher price. This is because there are more people who are interested in buying them, so the dealerships can charge more.
- **Reliability:** Some cars are more reliable than others. This means that they are less likely to break down, which is important for buyers who want a car that will last. Dealerships are more likely to sell reliable cars because they want to keep their customers happy.
- **Low mileage:** Cars with low mileage are in high demand because they are less likely to have any problems. This is because they have not been driven as much, so they have not been subjected to as much wear and tear.
- **Certified pre-owned (CPO):** CPO cars are inspected and certified by the manufacturer, which means that they are in good condition. This gives buyers peace of mind knowing that they are buying a quality car.

If you are looking for a used car, it is a good idea to consider buying one of the cars that are most popular with dealerships. These cars are more likely to be in demand, reliable, and have low mileage. They may also be certified pre-owned, which gives you even more peace of mind.

Here are some examples of cars that are popular with dealerships:

Sedans:

1. Toyota Camry
2. Honda Civic
3. Nissan Altima
4. Ford Fusion
5. Chevrolet Malibu
6. Hyundai Sonata
7. Volkswagen Jetta
8. BMW 3 Series
9. Mercedes-Benz C-Class
10. Audi A4

Coupes:

1. Ford Mustang
2. Chevrolet Camaro
3. Dodge Challenger
4. BMW 4 Series
5. Audi A5
6. Mercedes-Benz E-Class Coupe
7. Nissan 370Z

8. Honda Civic Coupe

9. Hyundai Genesis Coupe

10. Toyota 86

SUVs:

1. Ford Escape

2. Honda CR-V

3. Toyota RAV4

4. Chevrolet Equinox

5. Nissan Rogue

6. Jeep Grand Cherokee

7. Hyundai Tucson

8. Subaru Forester

9. Mazda CX-5

10. BMW X5

Pickup Trucks:

1. Ford F-150

2. Chevrolet Silverado 1500

3. Ram 1500

4. GMC Sierra 1500

5. Toyota Tacoma

6. Nissan Frontier

7. Honda Ridgeline

8. Chevrolet Colorado

9. Ford Ranger

10. Jeep Gladiator

Listen UP!

Your Motivation Minute

Listen up, car dealership champions! You're in the business of turning four wheels into dreams, of transforming transportation into exhilaration. You have the power to ignite imaginations, to create memories that will last a lifetime. Every car you sell represents a new chapter in someone's journey, a vehicle for their aspirations, and a conduit to adventure. Remember, you're not just selling cars; you're delivering possibilities, freedom, and joy. So, rev your engines, embrace the challenges, and keep your eyes on the road ahead. The world awaits your expertise, your passion, and your unwavering commitment to excellence. This is your time to shine, to make a difference one car at a time. Keep pushing forward, and remember that with every sale, you're not just selling a car; you're creating a connection, one that will drive smiles and build relationships. Get out there and show the world what you've got!

www.ingramcontent.com/pod-product-compliance
Lightning Source LLC
Chambersburg PA
CBHW070848220526
45466CB00005B/1931